I0412567

Wisdom
In
Words
Volume II

A Collection of Inspiring Quotations
For Every Day of the Year

Compiled by
Larry Rosenwinkel

WISDOM IN WORDS VOLUME II
Published by Carry-On Publishing Long Beach, CA

Acknowledgements and Thanks

Wow, here I am on volume two of Wisdom in Words, who woulduh thunk? And as I sit here, thinking about who to acknowledge and who to thank, the same names reappear, in addition to a few more. And while many things in life have changed, I still believe and know in my heart, we accomplish nothing alone. More and more, as I age, I find myself becoming frustrated with those who seemingly appear to have no awareness of others in their lives. Not a self-fullness but rather selfishness, because I know this book of quotes, and so much more, would not be possible without the love, help and support of many, adding to that, total strangers, who do what they do on a daily basis, to see that there's food in the grocery store when I go, gas at the pump and electricity flowing through the wires of my home, to name a few. To me, there's nothing more uplifting than going through each day with a grateful heart, most especially, when I find myself having a tough day, having a sense of gratefulness, always turns things around.

Always thankful to Mom & Dad (Shirley 1928-1998 and Wilmer Rosenwinkel 1928-2008); My sister, Lori Irvin; Jean F. Wakemen; Dr. Tonya Wood (El Woods – coolest shrink you ever met); Burleise Bailey; the whole damn Schram family (Dion, Hiro, Emi, Nick, Mayumi and Mari); Karen Leabo and our weekly kick-in-the-butt meetings; Micheal Deedon; Stacie Straw, Laura Gale, Karla Jones, Michael Cartwright and of course, my cat Valium.

Thank you, thank you, and thank you!
XXOO

Larry Rosenwinkel

Forward

Words have always and still do, fascinate me. Maybe that's why I was an English major in college. When I travel, I love to occupy my down time with word search puzzles. To me, words, whether spoken or written, possess great power. They can harm; they can do good, bring joy or sorrow; share love or hate, and while the spoken word is quite powerful, once something is put into writing, once those words have left the lips and made it to the page, there's no taking them back.

The amazing thing about words and their ability to invoke such power is they alone are void of emotion, it's only when the human element is added, do they then rise to their true potential.
Enter my background, education and personal relationship with the human experience. I was raised without little or no self-esteem in an environment that was more reactionary to life as opposed to being proactive toward it. While not religiously fanatic or zealous, the messages I received from church on Sundays and nine years of kindergarten thru 8th grade parochial school, told me I was bad, evil, born with sin and must spend the rest of my life repenting.

Philosophically speaking, I now know this is not necessarily the best way to get someone up and motivated about life. Add to the mix, during my —formativel years, a grandmother who was in and out of sanitariums and mental hospitals being treated for depression including electroshock therapy she would willingly request, and you have a young man who turns into an adult still looking for some sort of acceptance and comfort within himself, albeit, looking to the outside world to supply it.

Fortunately, I never turned to drugs or alcohol and while I now enjoy martinis, I didn't start drinking until I was of age. What I did do, however, was become a people pleaser. I worked hard at being loved although I was loved because of what I did for people and not for whom I was as a person. Over time, I learned I was, by nature, a giving person; I just had to learn to give to people who weren't takers. Eventually, after a little therapy and a whole bunch of self-help books, I connected with my own spirit finding strength and motivation in the paths others had followed, forming a more appropriate and healthier approach to my emotional and psychological self; therefore, a healthier path of my own. Who knew it would take me into my 40s to make that happen? And who knew in my 50s, I'd still be growing. The difference is I now get it. I accept life is ever changing; it's wonderful; it's difficult; it's joyous; it's painful – it's life.

And one of the greatest things in life, I believe, is nurturing and caring for ourselves and others with the second part of that unable to occur unless we've participated in the first. Love of self, leads to love of others but, some days, loving ourselves is not so easy. In our eyes, life just doesn't seem to be working with us. For me, that's where quotes come in. They're a little, daily reminder of who I know I am as well as who I know I want to become.

That said, the 365 quotes in this book were obtained randomly and published daily on Facebook. This was done without any aforethought or in relationship to any particular holiday, season or time of year. My goal was to just let them be, meaning, I "Googled" my way to a variety of quote sites bookmarking the ones that most inspired me and then, each morning, on a whim, would select a site and begin looking for a quote that —spoke to me. Some days, I would find one within a couple minutes; other days, I'd be at it for what seemed like half the morning.

Ultimately, though, I would find just the right one that for whatever reason for however and whomever I was that particular day, made me feel something. There were many days I didn't know what I needed to hear until I actually heard it. With no checklist or criteria in-hand, I would feel a connection to the words and what they said to me emotionally. For this reason, I have not set these 365 quotes to a year-long calendar, hoping you, too, will have a random, immediate connection to a quote as you flip through the book; therefore, making them more your own absorbing whatever insight and guidance you may need to hear that day.

I hope you enjoy the quotes I've selected and do well in making your life a little softer and a little brighter, filling it with additional strength and perseverance as you face the trials, tribulations, joys and wonderment of a richly, beautiful and engaged life.

"People, who fight fire with fire, usually end up with ashes".
Abigail Van Buren

"Once you label me you negate me". Soren Kierkegaard

"Failure is a path; not a destination". Robert Logan

"Character consists of what you do on the third and fourth tries".
James Albert Michener

"The life I touch for good or ill will touch another life, and that in turn another, until who knows where the trembling stops or in what far place my touch will be felt". Frederich Buechner

"Generosity means more than just giving. It also means to cooperate with others. The greatest act of generosity is to see beyond the weaknesses and mistakes of others, helping them to recognize their innate value". Innerspace

"Calm in quietude is not real calm. When you can be calm in the midst of activity, this is the true state of nature. Happiness in comfort is not real happiness. When you can be happy in the midst of hardship, then you see the true potential of the mind". Huanchu Daoren

"Your task is not to seek love, but merely to seek and find all the barriers within yourself that you have built against it". Rumi

"Without hope the heart breaks". Proverb

"The important thing is not to stop questioning. Curiosity has its own reason for existing. One cannot help but be in awe when he contemplates the mystery of eternity, of life, of the marvelous structure of reality. It is enough if one merely tries to comprehend a little of this mystery every day. Never lose a holy curiosity". Albert Einstein

"Always carry a flask of whiskey in case of snakebite and, furthermore, always carry a small snake". W.C. Fields

"You must train your intuition -- you must trust the small voice inside you which tells you exactly what to say, what to decide". Ingrid Bergman

"We are what we think. All that we are arises with our thoughts. With our thoughts, we make the world". Buddha

"A life lived in love will never be dull". Leo Buscaglia

"Insist on yourself; never imitate". Ralph Waldo Emerson

"It is one of the severest tests of friendship to tell your friend his faults. So to love a man that you cannot bear to see a stain upon him, and to speak painful truth through loving words, that is friendship". Henry Ward

"Peace comes from being able to contribute the best that we have, and all that we are, toward creating a world that supports everyone. But it is also securing the space for others to contribute the best that they have and all that they are". Hafsat Abiola

$\sim$

"Eventually I discovered for myself the utterly simple prescription for creativity; be intensely yourself. Don't try to be outstanding; don't try to be a success; don't try to do pictures for others to look at - just be yourself". Ralph Steiner

$\sim$

"Courage is not the absence of fear, but rather the judgment that something is more important than fear". Ambrose Redmoon

$\sim$

"Happiness is the absence of striving for happinessl. Chang-Tzu

$\sim$

"Conditions are never perfect "Someday" is a disease that will take your dreams to the grave with you. If it's important and you want to do it "eventually", just do it and correct course along the way". Tom Ferriss

"If your heart acquires strength, you will be able to remove blemishes from others without thinking evil of them". Mohandas K. Gandhi

"I have found that if you love life, life will love you back". Arthur Rubinstein

"Gratitude is a vaccine, an antitoxin, and an antiseptic". John Henry Jowett

"I know I have said a lot when I say 'You can do anything you want to do.' But I mean it... Blunder ahead with your personal view... The real work of art is the result of a magnificent struggle".
Robert Henri

"The only way to see a rainbow is to look through the rain".
Anonymous

"When you make a mistake, don't look back at it long. Take the reason of the thing into your mind and then look forward. Mistakes are lessons of wisdom. The past cannot be changed. The future is yet in your power". Hugh White

"The path to our destination is not always a straight one. We go down the wrong road, we get lost, we turn back. Maybe it doesn't matter which road we embark on. Maybe what matters is that we embark". Barbara Hall

"When you play it too safe, you take the biggest risk of your life. Time is the only wealth we're given". Barbara Sher

"Believe nothing just because a so-called wise person said it. Believe nothing just because a belief is generally held. Believe nothing just because it is said in ancient books. Believe nothing just because it is said to be of divine origin. Believe nothing just because someone else believes it. Believe only what you yourself test and judge to be true". Buddha

"Your imagination is your preview to life's coming attractions". Albert Einstein

"Laughter is an instant vacation". Milton Berle

"To know the road ahead, ask those coming back". Chinese proverb

"Ability is what you're capable of doing. Motivation determines what you do. Attitude determines how well you do it". Lou Holtz

"Don't bother to just be better than your contemporaries or predecessors. Try to be better than yourself". William Faulkner

"Nothing lasts forever. Not even your troubles". Arnold H. Glasgow

"When I hear someone say, —Life is hard, —I am always tempted to ask, —Compared to what?". Sydney J. Harris

"The mind is like a parachute. It doesn't work unless it's open". Frank Zappa

"What we must decide is how we are valuable rather than how valuable we are". Edgar K. Friedenberg

"Success is not the result of spontaneous combustion. You must set yourself on fire". Reggie Leach

"That's what learning is, after all; not whether we lose the game but how we lose and how we've changed because of it and what we take away from it that we never had before, to apply to other games. Losing, in a curious way, is winning". Richard Bach

"A lack of love, caring and compassion for others, is really a lack of love, caring and compassion for self". Larry Rosenwinkel

"If you ever find happiness by hunting for it, you will find it as the old woman did her lost spectacles, safe on her nose all the time". Josh Billings

"Many of our fears are tissue paper thin, and a single, courageous step would carry us through them". Brendan Francis

"Remember that not getting what you want is sometimes a wonderful stroke of luck". Dalai Lama

"I do not want the peace that passeth understanding; I want the understanding which bringeth peace". Helen Keller

"Everything happens for a reason, people change so that you can learn to let go, things go wrong so you can appreciate them when they're right, and sometimes good things fall apart so better things can come together". Marilyn Monroe

"Family isn't about whose blood you have. It's about who you care about". Trey Parker and Matt Stone

❧❧

"Having a role model in life is a great thing to have; one who provides us with direction and inspiration. However, we will forever be restricted by that person's limitations if we live within their boundaries. Be influenced, but set your own standards and develop your own principles, if you are ever to live beyond someone else's dreams". Jason Shahan

❧❧

"That's the risk you take if you change, that people you've been involved with won't like the new you. But other people who do will come along". Lisa Alther

❧❧

"If you pay attention at every moment, you form a new relationship to time. In some magical way, by slowing down, you become more efficient, productive, and energetic focusing without distraction directly on the task in front of you. Not only do you become immersed in the moment, you become that moment". Michael Ray

❧❧

"To understand the heart and mind of a person, look not at what he has already achieved, but what he aspires to". Khalil Gibran

"Perfectionism is not a quest for the best. It is a pursuit of the worst in ourselves, the part that tells us nothing that we do will ever be good enough – that we should try again". Julia Margaret Cameron

ও৵৶

"The art of being wise, is the art of knowing what to overlook".
William James

ও৵৶

"Of course, there is no formula for success except, perhaps, the unconditional acceptance of life and what it brings". Arthur Rubinstein

ও৵৶

"Realize deeply the present moment is all you ever have". Eckhart Tolle

ও৵৶

"To avoid situations in which you might make mistakes, may be the biggest mistake of all". Peter McWilliams

ও৵৶

"You may be deceived if you trust too much, but you will live in torment if you do not trust enough". Frank Crane

"I like nonsense – it wakes up the brain cells. Fantasy is a necessary ingredient in living. It's a way of looking at life through the wrong end of a telescope…and that enables you to laugh at all of life's realities". Theodor S. Geisel, a.k.a —Dr. Suess

"You cannot always control what goes on outside, but you can always control what goes on inside". Wayne Dyer

"The riches of life, the love and joy and exhilaration of life, can be found only with an upward look. This is an exciting world. It's cram-packed with opportunity. Great moments wait around every corner". Richard M. Devos

"When love and skill work together, expect a masterpiece". John Ruskin

"When the archer misses the mark, he turns and looks for the fault within himself. Failure to hit the bulls-eye is never the fault of the target. To improve your aim, improve yourself". Gilbert Arland

"A man should choose a friend who is better than himself. There are plenty of acquaintances in the world, but very few real friends". Chinese Proverb

"Don't be pushed by your problems. Be lead by your dreams". Anonymous

"The truth is that our finest moments are most likely to occur when we are feeling deeply uncomfortable, unhappy, or unfulfilled. For it is only in such moments, propelled by our discomfort, that we are likely to step out of our ruts and start searching for different ways or truer answers". M. Scott Peck

"Life is a gift, and it offers us the privilege, opportunity and responsibility to give something back by becoming more". Anthony Robbins

"The chief danger in life is that you may take too many precautions". Alfred Adler

"To acquire knowledge, one must study; to acquire wisdom, one must observe". Marilyn vos Savant

"What most people need to learn in life, is how to love people and use things instead of using people and loving things". Anonymous

"I keep the telephone of my mind open to peace, harmony, love, health and abundance. Then, whenever doubt, anxiety or fear try to call me, they will keep getting a busy signal and soon they will forget my number". Edith Armstrong

"The beginning of love is to let those we love be perfectly themselves and not twist them to fit our own image; otherwise, we love only the reflection of ourselves we find in them". Thomas Merton

"Death ends a life; not a relationship". Mitch Albom

"To understand the meaning of life, begin with understanding the meaning of your own". Larry Rosenwinkel

"We can only be said to be alive in those moments when our hearts are conscious of our treasures". Thornton Wilder

"The greater part of our happiness or misery depends on our disposition and not our circumstances. We carry the seeds of one or the other about with us in our minds wherever we go". Martha Washington

"I do not believe that sheer suffering teaches. If suffering along taught, all the world would be wise since everyone suffers. To suffering, must be added mourning, understanding, patience, love, openness and the willingness to remain vulnerable". Joseph Addison

"Guard well within yourself that treasure, kindness. Know how to give without hesitation, how to lose without regret, how to acquire without meanness". George Sand

"All life is an experiment. The more experiments you make the better". Ralph Waldo Emerson

"I can only give my best to others, when I am in touch with the best in myself". Innerspace

"Don't seek, don't search, don't ask, don't knock, don't demand – relax. If you relax, it comes. If you relax, it's there. If you relax, you start vibrating with it". Osho

❧❧

"The world is wide, and I will not waste my life in friction, when it can be turned into momentum". Frances Willard

❧❧

"Friendship is born at the moment when one person says to another: —What! you too? I thought I was the only one". C.S. Lewis

❧❧

"When they discover the center of the universe, a lot of people will be disappointed to discover they are not it". Bernard Baily

❧❧

"Those who wish to sing, always find a song". Proverb

❧❧

"Hope is not the conviction that something will turn out well, but the certainty that something makes sense regardless of how it turns out". Vaclav Havel

❧❧

"Everyone marches to the beat of a different drummer. Fall in love with your own rhythm". Larry Rosenwinkel

"No one knows your capability, as well as you do. No one knows how big you can dream and no one knows how far you can go. You, like water, can seek and reach your own level". Lynne Cox

"Each moment of every day, every action of living, poses the question: how it might be lived differently, more truthfully and respectfully". Markuz Wernlie Saito

"Too many of us are not living our dreams, because we are living our fears". Les Brown

"Say yes to life, even though you know it may devour you". Stephen Larsen

"The more I traveled the more I realized fear makes strangers of people who should be friends". Shirley Maclaine

"What you fear for your children most, sadly enough, has nothing to do with them and everything to do with you. If and when you come to terms with your childhood, only then, will you enrich theirs". Larry Rosenwinkel

"To awaken in a strange town is one of the most pleasant sensations in the world". Freya Stark

"Feeling grateful or appreciative of someone or something in your life, actually attracts more of the things you appreciate and value in your life". Northrup Christiane

"My favorite thing is to go where I've never been". Diane Arbus

"I have learned life may not always be easy, but it is always worth living". Melanie Rice

"Many of us spend half our lives wishing for things we could have if we didn't spend half our time wishing". Alexander Woollcot

"We never really grow up; we just learn how to behave in public". Bryan White

∽∾

"Given the choice between two theories, choose the one that is funnier". Anonymous

∽∾

"Decorate yourself from the inside out". Andrei Turnhollow

∽∾

"Things that were hard to bear are sweet to remember". Seneca the Younger

∽∾

"Only as high as I reach can I grow, only as far as I seek can I go, only as deep as I look can I see, only as much as I dream can I be". Karen Ravn

"Sometimes, I think the surest sign that intelligent life exists elsewhere in the universe is that none of it has tried to contact us". Bill Watterson

"We grow because we struggle, we learn and overcome". R. C. Allen

"The river of life is constantly bringing you ideas, people, situations; each one is an opportunity to be enriched or enrich others, and to learn. Change is the play of the universe as it entertains us with the biggest light and sound show of all time. Why not sit back and enjoy the show!". Innerspace

"The price of the democratic way of life is a growing appreciation of people's differences not merely as tolerable but as the essence of a rich and rewarding human experience". Jerome Nathanson

"Heal the past, live the present, dream the future". Anonymous

"You have to grow from the inside out. None can teach you, none can make you spiritual. There is no other teacher but your own soul". Swami Vivekananda

"Real joy comes not from ease or riches or from the praise of men, but from doing something worthwhile". Sir Wilfred Grenfell

တတ

"Time Flies. It's up to you to be the navigator". Robert Orben

တတ

"Dreams are answers to questions we haven't yet figured out how to ask". Fox Mulder, —The X-Files

တတ

"There is nothing worse than aggressive stupidity". Johann Wolfgang von Goethe

တတ

"There is only one success — to be able to spend your life in your own way". Christopher Morley

တတ

"The most wasted of all days is one without laughter". E. E. Cummings

"Don't bend; don't water it down; don't try to make it logical; don't edit your own soul according to fashion. Rather, follow your most intense obsessions mercilessly". Frank Kafka

❧

"A discovery is said to be an accident meeting a prepared mind'. Albert Szent- Gyorgyi

❧

"Trouble is only opportunity in work clothes". Henry J. Kaiser

❧

"Life is either a daring adventure or nothing. To keep our faces toward change, and behave life free spirits in the presence of fate is strength undefeatable". Helen Keller

❧

"When I let go of what I am, I become what I might be". John Heider

❧

"I am convinced that life in a physical body, is meant to be an ecstatic experience". Shakti Gawain

"Never bear more than one trouble at a time. Some people bear three kinds, all they have had, all they have now and all they expect to have". Edward Everett Hale

"Men are not prisoners of fate, but only prisoners of their own minds". Franklin D. Roosevelt

"One's dignity may be assaulted, vandalized and cruelly mocked, but cannot be taken away unless it is surrendered". Michael J. Fox

"One resolution I have made and try always to keep, is this: To rise above the little things". John Burroughs

"And above all, watch with glittering eyes the whole world around you, because the greatest gifts are always hidden in the most unlikely places. Those who do not believe in magic, will never find it". Roald Dahl

"The past is a source of knowledge, and the future is a source of hope. Love of the past, implies faith in the future". Stephen Ambrose in Fast Company

"If there is no struggle, there is no progress". Frederick Douglass

"You create your opportunities by asking for them|". Patty Hansen

"Make no little plans, they have no magic to stir men's blood. Make big plans, aim high in hope and work". Daniel H. Burnham

"You cannot test courage cautiously". Annie Dillard

"You are today where your thoughts have brought you; you will be tomorrow where your thoughts take you". Ralph Waldo Emerson

"The worst loneliness is not to be comfortable with yourself". Mark Twain

"It is a curious thought, but it is only when you see people looking ridiculous that you realize just how much you love them". Agatha Christie

"When you look for the good in others, you find the good in yourself". Anonymous

"Excess on occasion is exhilarating. It prevents moderation from acquiring the deadening effect of a habit". W. Somerset Maugham

"Time engranes our faces with the tears we have not shed". Natalie Cellford Barney

"Don't do what you want. Do what you don't want. Do what you're trained not to want. Do the things that scare you most ". Chuck Palahniuk

"After all, it is those who have a deep and real inner life who are best able to deal with the irritating details of outer life". Evelyn Underhill

"The past is to be respected and acknowledged, but not to be worshiped. It is our future in which we will find our greatness". Pierre Trudeau

"I am not a quitter. I will fight until I drop. It is just a matter of having some faith in the fact that as long as your are able to draw breath in the universe, you have a chance". Cicely Tyson

"Among those whom I like and admire, I can find no common denominator, but among those whom I love, I can: All of them make me laugh". W. H. Auden

"There is a loftier ambition than merely to stand high in the world. It is to stoop down and lift mankind a little higher". Henry Van Dyke

"I sometimes think expect too much from Christmas Day. We try to crowd it into the long arrears of kindliness and humanity of the whole year. As for me, I like to take my Christmas a little at a time all through the year. And thus, I drift along into the holiday – let them take me over unexpectedly – waking up some fine morning and suddenly saying to myself: —Why, this is Christmas Day". David Grayson

"We inherit nothing truly, but what our actions make us worthy of". George Chapman

"Failure is an event, never a person". William D. Brown

"The secret of getting ahead, is getting started. The secret of getting started, is breaking your overwhelming, complex tasks into small, manageable tasks, and then starting on the first one". Mark Twain

"If we did all the things we are capable of doing, we would literally astonish ourselves". Thomas A. Edison

"If we listened to our intellect, we'd never have a love affair. We'd never have a friendship. We'd never go into business, because we'd be cynical. Well, that's nonsense. You've got to jump off cliffs all the time and build your wings on the way down". Ray Bradbury

"We spend January 1 walking through our lives, room by room, drawing up a list of work to be done, cracks. Maybe this year to balance the list, we ought walk through the rooms of our lives, not looking for flaws, but for potential". Ellen Goodman

"Success is more a function of consistent common sense that it is of genius". An Wang

"To become acquainted with kindness, one must prepare to learn new things and feel new things. Kindness is more than a philosophy of the mind, it is a philosophy of the spirit". Robert J. Furey

"Feeling gratitude and not expressing it, is like wrapping a present and not giving it". William Arthur Ward

"From the backstabbing co-worker, to the meddling relative, you are in charge of how you react to people and events in your life. You can either give negativity power over your life, or you can choose happiness instead. Take control and choose to focus on what's important in your life. Those who cannot live fully usually become destroyers of life". Anais Nin

"It's not that some people have willpower and some don't. It's that some people are ready to change and others are not'. James Gordon

"We are all stars, and we all deserve to twinkle". Marilyn Monroe

"To find something you can enjoy, is far better than finding something you can possess". Glen Holm

"I really don't think life is about the I-could-have-beens. Life is only about the I-tried-to-do. I don't mind the failure, but I can't imagine that I'd forgive myself if I didn't try". Nikki Giovann

"Failure is not reaching your goal, but in not having a goal to reach". Benjamin Mays

"Courage and perseverance have a magical talisman, before which difficulties disappear and obstacles vanish into thin air". John Quincy Adams

"We are cups, constantly and quietly being filled. The trick is, knowing how to tip ourselves over and let the beautiful stuff out". Ray Bradbury

"Hate is a disease. It is fear's messenger and it makes us do terrible things in a shadow of our better selves, of what we could be". Colin Farrell

"Progress always involves risks. You can't steal second base and keep your foot on first". Frederick Wilcox

"I long to accomplish great and noble task, but it is my chief duty to accomplish tasks as though they were great and noble. The world is moved along not only by the mighty shoves of its heroes, but by the aggregate of the tiny pushes of each honest worker". Helen Keller

"I have had dreams and I have had nightmares, but I have conquered my nightmares because of my dreams". Jonas Salk

"You never lose by loving. You always lose by holding back". Barbara De Angelis

"Happiness cannot be traveled to, owned, earned, won or consumed. Happiness is the spiritual experience of living every minute with love, grace and gratitude". Denis Waitley

"If you realized how powerful your thoughts are, you would never think a negative thought". Peace Pilgrim

"Human beings, by changing the inner aspects of their minds, can change the outer aspects of their lives!". William James

"Love many things for therein lies the true strength, and whosoever loves much performs much, and can accomplish much, and what is done in love, is done well". Vincent Van Gogh

"This is the final test of a gentleman: his respect for those who can be of no possible value to him". William Lyon Phelps

"It's a sad day when you find out that it's not accident or time or fortune, but just yourself that kept things from you". Lillian Hellman

"In the spiritual life, nowhere do our ideals meet the actual more truly than in how we relate to each other, in how we make, sustain, and are friends". James Ishmael Ford

"By believing passionately in something that does not yet exist, we create it". Nikos Kazantzakis

"It isn't what you have or who you are, or where you are, or what you are doing that makes you happy. It's what you think about". Dale Carnegie

"We can either live our lives preparing for the worst or living for the best. It's a choice". Larry Rosenwinkel

ভ্ৰৎ

"Small acts when multiplied by millions of people, can change the world". Howard Zinn

ভ্ৰৎ

"Slow down and enjoy life. It's not only the scenery you miss by going too fast, you also miss the sense of where you are going and why". Eddie Cantor

ভ্ৰৎ

"I would rather have a mind opened with wonder, than one closed by belief'. Gerry Spencer

ভ্ৰৎ

"Opportunity dances with those who are ready on the dance floor". H. Jackson Brown

ভ্ৰৎ

"Life is meaningless only if we allow it to be. Each of us has the power to give life meaning, to make our time and our bodies and our words instruments of love and hope". Tom Head

"The manager accepts the status quo; the leader challenges it". Warren Bennis

ॐ

"Why are we scared to die? Do any of us remember being scared when we were born". Trevor Kay

ॐ

"It is better to hang out with people better than you. Pick out associates whose behavior is better than yours and you'll drift in that direction'. Warren Buffet

ॐ

"Dream and give yourself permission to envision a you that you choose to be". Joy Page

ॐ

"We cannot live for ourselves alone. Our lives are connected by a thousand invisible thread, and along those fibers. our actions run as causes and return to us as a result‖". Herman Melville

ॐ

"We do not quit playing because we get old, we get old because we quit playing". Oliver Wendell

"We don't see things as they are; we see them as we are".
Anonymous

❧

"In prosperity, our friends know us; in adversity, we know our friends". John Churton Collins

❧

"One of the greatest moments in anybody's developing experience, is when he no longer tries to hide from himself, but determines to get acquainted with himself as he really is". Norman Vincent Peale

❧

"The soul is not where it lives, but where it loves". Proverb

❧

"Ineffective people live day after day with unused potential. They experience synergy only in small, peripheral ways in their lives. But creative experiences can be produced regularly, consistently, almost daily in people's lives. It requires enormous personal security, openness and a spirit of adventure". Stephen R. Covey

❧

"Our aspirations are our possibilities". Samuel Johnson

"Life is all about movement. For we humans, bringing together where we were with where we are, is what makes us whole". Larry Rosenwinkel

"When you move amidst the world of sense, free from attachment and aversions alike, there comes the peace in which all sorrows end, and you live in the wisdom of the self". Bhagavad Gita

"Act as if you have already achieved your goal, and it is yours". Dr. Anthony

"Fear is the main source of superstition and one of the main sources of cruelty. To conquer fear is the beginning of wisdom". Bertrand Russell

"It's the soul's duty to be loyal to its own desires. It must abandon itself to its master passion". Rebecca West

"We have but one life to live, my suggestion, ride it hard and put it away wet". Anonymous

"If you can't return a favor, pass it on". Louise Brown

"In all human affairs there are efforts, and there are results, and the strength of effort is the measure of the results". James Allen

"What comes from the heart, goes to the heart". Samuel Taylor Coleridge

"One of the things my parents taught me, and I'll always be grateful for the gift, is to not ever let anyone else define me". Wilma Mankiller

"Success comes from knowing that you did your best to become the best that you are capable of becoming". John Wooden

"Too many people are thinking of security instead of opportunity. They seem to be more afraid of life than death". James F. Byrnes

"The more anger towards the past you carry in your heart, the less capable you are of loving in the present". Barbara de Angelis

"The purpose of life is a life of purpose". Robert Byrne

"Listening is a magnetic and strange thing, a creative force. The friends who listen to us are the ones we move toward. When we are listened to, it creates us, makes us unfold and expand". Karl Menninger

∽◆∾

"It is only possible to live happily ever after on a day to day basis". Margaret Bonnano

∽◆∾

"Have patience with all things, but chiefly have patience with yourself. Do not lose courage in considering your own imperfections but instantly set about remedying them — every day begin the task anew". Saint Francis de Sales

∽◆∾

"I can be changed by what happens to me, but I refuse to be reduced by it". Maya Angelou

∽◆∾

"I wish I could show you when you are lonely or in darkness, the astonishing light of your own being". Hafiz of Persia

∽◆∾

"Life itself is the proper binge". Julia Child

"If you always do what you always did, you'll always get what you always got". Anonymous

❧

"Life's challenges are not supposed to paralyze you, they're supposed to help you discover who you are". Bernice Johnson Reagon

❧

"Practice easing your way along. Do your best; take it as it comes. You can handle anything if you think you can. Just keep your cool and your sense of humor". Smiley Blanton

❧

"You grow up the day you have your first real laugh at yourself". Ethel Barrymore

❧

"I cannot believe the purpose of life is to be ―happy‖. I think the purpose of life is to be useful, to be responsible, to be compassionate. It is, above all, to matter and to count, to stand for something, to have made some difference that you have lived at all". Leo C. Rosten

❧

"The ultimate lesson we all have to learn, is unconditional love, which includes not only others but ourselves as well". Elizabeth Kubler-Ross

"Establishing goals is an all right thing if you don't let them deprive you of interesting detours". Doug Larson

"If one is lucky, a solitary fantasy can totally transform one million realities". Maya Angelou

"Let yourself be silently drawn by the stronger pull of what you really love". Rumi

"When nothing goes right, go left". Anonymous

"Today you are you. That is truer than true. No one alive is youer than you". Dr. Seuss

"You never know how strong you are until being strong is the only choice you have". Author unknown

"Our prime purpose in life is to help others. And if you can't help them, at least don't hurt them". Henry David Thoreau

"It is not work that kills men, it is worry. Work is healthy; you can hardly put more on a man than he can bear. But worry is rust upon the blade. It is not movement that destroys the machinery, but friction". Henry Ward Beecher

"Action expresses priorities". Mohandas K. Gandhi

"There is never enough time to do everything, but there is always enough time to do the most important thing". Brain Tracy

"I could not at any age, be content to take my place by the fireside and simply look on. Life was meant to be lived. Curiosity must be kept alive. Never for whatever reason, turn his back on life". Eleanor Roosevelt

"Sometimes the dreams that come true are the dreams you never even knew you had". Anonymous

"The problem is not that there are problems. The problem is expecting otherwise and thinking that having problems is a problem". Theodore Rubin

"Better hazard once than always be in fear". Thomas Fuller

"When I thought I couldn't go on, I forced myself to keep going. My success is based on persistence, not luck". Estee Lauder

"The only place where your dreams become impossible is in your own thinking'. Robert H. Schuller

"Forget mistakes. Forget failure. Forget everything except what you're going to do now and do it. Today, is your lucky day‖". Will Durant

"Life begins at the end of your comfort zone". Neale Donald Walsch

"We lift ourselves by our thought. We climb upon our vision of ourselves. If you want to enlarge your life, you must first enlarge your thought of it and of yourself. Hold the ideal of yourself as you long to be, always everywhere". Orison Swett Marden

"Life is meaningless only if we allow it to be. Each of us has the power to give life meaning, to make our time and our bodies and our words into instruments of love and hope". Tom Head

"If you think about disaster, you will get it. Brood about death and you hasten your demise. Think positively and masterfully, with confidence and faith, and life becomes more secure, more fraught with action, richer in achievement and experience". Eddie Rickenbacker

"I do not think of God theistically, that is, as a being, supernatural in power, who dwells beyond the limits of my world. I rather experience God as the source of life willing me to live fully, the source of love calling me to love wastefully and to borrow a phrase from the theologian, Paul Tillich, as the Ground of being, calling me to be all that I can be". John Shelby Spong

"A person's world is only as big as their heart". Lynne Cox

"Could a greater miracle take place than for us to look through each other's eyes for an instant?". Henry David Thoreau

'Tough times never last but tough people do". John Thomas Salley

"Life is too short, so kiss slowly, laugh insanely, love truly and forgive quickly". Anonymous

ஒ◦ஓ

"The great pleasure in life is doing what people say you cannot do". Walter Bageho

ஒ◦ஓ

"Life is too short to spend your precious time trying to convince a person who wants to live in gloom and doom otherwise. Give lifting that person your best shot, but don't hang around long enough for his or her bad attitude to pull you down. Instead, surround yourself with optimistic people". Anonymous

ஒ◦ஓ

"Reexamine all that you have been told in school, or in church or in any book. Dismiss whatever insults your soul". Walt Whitman

ஒ◦ஓ

"Believe, deep down in your heart, that you're destined to do great things". Joe Paterno

ஒ◦ஓ

"All the art of living lies in a fine mingling of letting go and holding on". Henry Ellis

"In life you find that one of the most desirable qualities you can find in a person is flexibility. The ability to change with changing times, to face adversity with the same attitude one would have in facing victory". A Guide to a Happy Life

"The most important trip you may take in life is meeting people halfway". Henry Boye

"A life of reaction is a life of slavery, intellectually and spiritually. One must fight for a life of action, not reaction". Rita Mae Brown

"If you really want to change your thinking and your life, make a decision today to begin associating, in every area of your life, with other men and women whom you admire, respect, and look up to'. Brian Tracy

"Of course there is not formula for success except, perhaps, an unconditional acceptance of life and what it brings". Arthur Rubinstein

"We lift ourselves by our thought. We climb upon our vision of ourselves. If you want to enlarge your life, you must first enlarge your thought of it and of yourself. Hold the ideal of yourself as you long to be, always everywhere.". Orison Swett Marden

"When life gives you a hundred reasons to cry, show life that you have a thousand reasons to smile". Unknown

"At first, I only laughed at myself. Then I noticed that life itself is amusing. I've been in a generally good mood ever since". Marilyn Vos Savant

"Tomorrow is the most important thing in life, comes into us at midnight very clean. It's perfect when it arrives and it puts itself in our hands. It hopes we've learned something from yesterday". John Wayne

"Life is better when you are happy. But life is at its best when other people are happy because of you. Be inspired & share your smile with everyone". Unknown

"Be where you are; otherwise you will miss your life". Buddha

"My great mistake, the fault for which I can't forgive myself, is that one day I ceased my obstinate pursuit of my own individuality!".
Oscar Wilde

ରୁକ୍ଦ

"Some experiences simply do not translate. You have to go to know". Kobi Yamada

ରୁକ୍ଦ

"It doesn't matter how long we may have been stuck in a sense of our limitations. If we go into a darkened room and turn on the light, it doesn't matter if the room has been dark for a day, a week, or ten thousand years — we turn on the light and it is illuminated. Once we control our capacity for love and happiness, the light has been turned on". Sharon Salzberg

ରୁକ୍ଦ

"When you choose to be pleasant and positive in the way you treat others, you have also chosen, in most cases, how you are going to be treated by others". Zig Ziglar

ରୁକ୍ଦ

"Good instincts usually tell you what to do long before your head has figured it out". Michael Burke

ରୁକ୍ଦ

"All glory comes from daring to begin". Eugene F. Ware

"Whatever you do, even when you are in down condition, don't lose your hopes. Whatever your hopes are, they will guide you to your success in life". Lemy Yusento

"We all have our own life to pursue, our own kind of dream to be weaving. And we all have some power to make wishes come true, as long as we keep believing". Louisa May Alcott

"The more you care the stronger you can be". Jim Rohn

"That best portion of a good man's life, his little, nameless, unremembered acts of kindness and of love". William Wordsworth

"Some people are always grumbling because roses have thorns; I am thankful that thorns have roses". Alphonse Karr

"Joy is the best makeup". Anne Lamott

"Good people are good because they've come to wisdom through failure. We get very little wisdom from success, you know". William Saroyan

"Life is like photography. You use the negatives to develop".
Anonymous

"It's not who you are that holds you back. It's who you think you're
not". Anonymous

"Not a shred of evidence exists in favor of the idea that life is
serious". Brendan Gill

"Yearn for the impossible". Johann Wolfgang von Goethe

"As I go through all kinds of feelings and experiences in my
journey through life — delight, surprise, chagrin, dismay — I hold
this question as a guiding light: —What do I really need right now
to be happy? What I come to over and over again is that only
qualities as vast and deep as love, connection and kindness will
really make me happy in any sort of enduring way". Sharon
Salzberg

"When you arise in the morning, think of what a precious privilege it is to be alive – to breathe, to think, to enjoy, to love". Marcus Aurelius

"Leap and the net will appear".   Julie Cameron

"Happiness is not in our circumstances, but in ourselves. It is not something we see, like a rainbow, or feel, like the heat of a fire. Happiness is something we are". John B. Sheerin

"People usually consider walking on water or in thin air a miracle. But I think the real miracle is not to walk either on water or in thin air, but to walk on earth. Every day we are engaged in a miracle which we don't even recognize: a blue sky, white clouds, green leaves, the black, curious eyes of a child — our own two eyes. All is a miracle".   Thich Hanh

"Life is not a matter of having good cards, but of playing a poor hand well".   Robert Louis Stevenson

"When you live your life with an appreciation of coincidences and their meanings, you connect with the underlying field of infinite possibilities". Deepak Chopra

"My will shall shape the future. Whether I fail or succeed shall be no man's doing but my own. I am the force; I can clear any obstacle before me or I can be lost in the maze. My choice; my responsibility; win or lose, only I hold the key to my destiny".
Elaine Maxwell

"Affirm continuously to yourself: I am in the right place, at the right time, for the right purpose". Ursula Roberts

"Life is made up of little things. It is very rarely that an occasion is offered for doing a great deal at once. True greatness consists in being great in the little things|". Charles Simmons

"People become really quite remarkable when they start thinking that they can do things. When they believe in themselves they have the first secret of success". Norman Vincent Peale

"If you are distressed by anything external, the pain is not due to the thing itself, but to your estimate of it; and this you have the power to revoke at any moment". Marcus Aurelius

"To get up each morning with the resolve to be happy is to set our own conditions to the events of each day. To do this is to condition circumstances instead of being conditioned by the". Ralph Waldo Trine

"One should guard against preaching to young people success in the customary form as the main aim in life. The most important motive for work in school and in life is pleasure in work, pleasure in its result and the knowledge of the value of the result to the community". Albert Einstein

"It takes a lot of courage to release the familiar and seemingly secure, to embrace the new. But there is no real security in what is no longer meaningful. There is more security in the adventurous and exciting, for in movement there is life, and in change there is power". Alan Cohen

"Wherever you are, be there totally. If you find your here and now intolerable and it makes you unhappy, you have three options: remove yourself from the situation, change it, or accept it totally". Eckhart Tolle

"People take different roads seeking fulfillment and happiness. Just because they're not on your road, doesn't mean they've gotten lost". H. Jackson Brown, Jr.

"Every thought is a seed. If you plant crab apples, don't count on harvesting Golden Delicious". Bill Meyer

"Being defeated is often a temporary condition. Giving up is what makes it permanent". Marlene vos Savant

"The brain created it; therefore, the brain can change it". Anonymous

"If you will call your troubles experiences, and remember that every experience develops some latent force within you, you will grow vigorous and happy, however adverse your circumstances may seem to be". John Heywood

"Generally, appreciation means some blend of thankfulness, admiration, approval, and gratitude. In the financial world, something that —appreciates‖ grows in value. With the power tool of appreciation, you get the benefit of both perspectives: as you learn to be consistently thankful and approving, your life will grow in value". Doc Childre and Howard Martin

"Sometimes you have to let go to see if there was anything worth holding on to‖". Unknown

"It is so important to believe in yourself. Believe that you can do it, under any circumstances. Because if you believe you can, then you really will. That belief just keeps you searching for the answers, and then pretty soon you get It". Wally Amos

"It goes with your everywhere you go. It is on display at work and at home. People around you are affected by it. It has no shape, color, or size, yet its impact on your life is profound. What is it? Your attitude!". Lucy MacDonald

"Failure is simply the opportunity to begin again, this time more intelligently". Henry Ford

"Detachment involves present-moment living – living in the here and now. We allow life to happen instead of forcing and trying to control it. We relinquish regrets over the past and fears about the future. We make the most of each day". Melody Beattie

"Everything is material for the seed of happiness, if you look into it with inquisitiveness and curiosity. The future is completely open, and we are writing it moment to moment. There always is the potential to create an environment of blame -- or one that is conducive to loving-kindness". Pema Chodron

"You can't punish yourself into change. You can't whip yourself into shape. But you can love yourself into well-being". Susan Skye

"I believe that imagination is stronger than knowledge — myth is more potent than history — dreams are more powerful than facts — hope always triumphs over experience — laughter is the cure for grief — love is stronger than deathǀ". Robert Fulghum

"Pursue some path, however narrow and crooked, in which you can walk with love and reverence". Henry David Thoreau

"If we fall asleep every night counting and acknowledging our blessings — we give permission for *The Universe* to keep bringing them. When we show appreciation and give thanks for those blessings, we invite more of the same into our personal world". Chelle Thompson

"The problem with doing nothing, is not knowing when you're finished". Benjamin Franklin

"The Wright brothers flew through the smoke screen of impossibility". Dorothea Brande

"You're alive. That means you have infinite potential. You can do anything, make anything, dream anything. If you change the world, the world will change". Neil Gaiman

"We all have two choices; we can make a living or we can design a life". Jim Rohn

"Follow you heart, but be quiet for awhile first. Ask questions, then feel the answer, learn to trust your heart". Anonymous

"It's not denial. I'm just selective about the reality I accept". Calvin and Hobbes

"Don't bother just to be better than your contemporaries or predecessors. Try to be better than yourself|". William Faulkner

"Expecting the world to treat you fairly because you are a good person is a little like expecting the bull not to attack you because you are a vegetarian". Dennis Wholey

"If you focus on results, you will never change. If you focus on change, you will get results". Jack Dixon

"You will never find time for anything. If you want time, you must make it". Charles Bixton

"Love is but the discovery of ourselves in others, and the delight in the recognition". Alexander Smith

"I love this holiday (4th of July). Why? You ask? Cause its one of the few holiday's in this country where EVERYONE is invited to play. I love inclusion. Let's eat, drink, and be merry". Michael Cartwright

"Happiness comes of the capacity to feel deeply, to enjoy simply, to think freely, to risk life, to be needed". Storm Jameson

"Living the past is a dull and lonely business; looking back strains the neck muscles, causing you to bump into people not going your way". Edna Ferber

"Nobody trips over mountains. It is the small pebble that causes you to stumble. Pass all the pebbles in your path and you will find you have crossed the mountain". Unknown

"The question isn't who is going to let me; it's who is going to stop me". Ayn Rand

"You cannot be lonely if you like the person you're alone with". Wayne Dyer

"If you could travel back in time to the present moment, what would you do differently?". Robert Brault

"You life is your message to the world, make it inspiring". Lorrin L. Lee

"Believe that life is worth living and your belief will create the fact". William James

"The fact that I can plant a seed and it becomes a flower, share a bit of knowledge and it becomes another's, smile at someone and receive a smile in return, are to me continual spiritual exercises". Leo Buscaglia

"Mistakes are a fact of life. It is the response to error that counts". Nikki Giovanni

"There are two great days in a person's life – the day we are born and the day we discover why". William Barclay

"Be inspired with the belief that life is a great and noble calling; not a mean and groveling thing that we are to shuffle through as we can, but an elevated and lofty destiny".   William E. Gladstone

"You cannot discover the purpose of life by asking someone else –
the only way you'll ever get the right answer is by asking yourself".
Terri Guillemets

"Your vision will become clear only when you look into your heart.
Who looks outside, dreams. Who looks inside, awakens". Carl Jung

"An ideal life does not exist; but a happy one can be attained".
Greg Evens

"Aim for success, not perfection. Never give up your right to be
wrong, because then you will lose the ability to learn new things
and move forward with your life. Remember that fear always lurks
behind perfectionism". David M. Burns

"Above all challenge yourself. You may well surprise yourself at
what strengths you have, what you can accomplish". Cecile
Springer

"Someone's opinion of you does not have to become your reality".
Les Brown

"Every person, all the events of your life are there because you have drawn them there. What you choose to do with them is up to you". Richard Bach

"Courage is what it takes to stand up and speak; courage is also what it takes to sit down and listen". Winston Churchill

"It is difficult to say what is impossible, for the dream of yesterday is the hope of today and the reality of tomorrow". Robert H. Goddard

"If there is any peace it will come through being, not knowing". Henry Miller

"The natural flights of the human mind are not from pleasure to pleasure but from hope to hope".   Dr. Johnson

"Other people and things can stop you temporarily. You're the only one who can do it permanently". Zig Ziglar

"Life … is not about how fast you run or even with what degree of grace. It's about perseverance, about staying on your feet and slogging forward no matter what". Dean Koontz

"As the sea is beautiful not only in calm but also in storm, so is happiness found not only in peace but also in strife". Ivan Panin

"The quality of our expectations determines the quality of our actions". Andre Godin

"Knowledge is learning something new every day. Wisdom is letting go of something every day". Zen Proverb

"Sometimes, you need to step outside, get some air, and remind yourself who you are and who you want to be". Anonymous

"It's impossible, said pride. —It's risky, said experience. —It's pointless, said reason. —Give it a try, whispered the heart". Anonymous

"It is impossible to live without failing at something, unless you live so cautiously that you might as well not lived at all, in which case, you fail by default".   J.K. Rowlling

"Sometimes I pretend to be normal, but it gets boring so I go back to being me". Allegra Villella

"To accomplish great things, we must not only act, but also dream; not only plan, but also believe". Anatole France

"Life takes on meaning when you become motivated, take on goals, and charge after them in an unstoppable manner".   Les Brown

"Everything you are, and everything you have, started as a thought in your mind. Your body is merely there to manifest physically that which the mind tells it to do. Everything starts with you telling the mind what you desire". Thomas D. Willhite

"Don't let the fear of the time it will take to accomplish something stand in the way of your doing it. The time will pass anyway; we might just as well put that passing time to the best possible use". Earl Nightingale

"Experience is not what happens to a man; it's what a man does with what happens to him". Aldous Huxley

"Being different is one of the most beautiful things on earth, embrace your —you‖ ness". A. Edwards

"People will always say that you're going the wrong way when it's simply a way of your own". Angelina Jolie

"You leave old habits behind by starting out with the thought, _I release the need for this in my life". Dr. Wayne Dyer

"Think positive thoughts, intensely. Grow enthusiastic images, boldly. Speak only wonderful words to yourself, constantly. Feel fantastic, NOW! This colors your view of the world. Like a magnet, you attract the resources necessary to manifest the world you desire". Mark Victor Hanson and Robert Allen

"The individual has always had to struggle to keep from being overwhelmed by the tribe. If you try it, you will be lonely often, and sometimes frightened. But no price is too high to pay for the privilege of owning yourself.". Friedrich Nietzsche

❧❧

"In essence, if we want to direct our lives, we must take control of our consistent actions. It's not what we do once in a while that shapes our lives, but what we do consistently'. Tony Robbins

❧❧

"If you worry about what might be, and wonder what might have been, you will ignore what is". Anonymous

❧❧

"Success means having the courage, the determination, and the will to become the person you believe you were meant to be". George Sheehan

❧❧

"If you're paying attention to your own life, nothing in someone else's will come as a surprise". Larry Rosenwinkel

"Be grateful for setbacks, they are opportunities for even more improvements‖". Lorrin Lee

"Sometimes you have to let go to see if there was anything worth holding on to".   Unknown

Larry's Favorites

A Self-Help Reading List

The Seat of the Soul by Gary Zukav

In the Meantime by Iyanla Vanzant

The Power of Now by Eckhart Tolle

Co-dependent No More by Melody Beattie

The Language of Letting Go by Melody Beattie

Don't Sweat the Small Stuff by Richard Carlson

The Secrets of Self-Esteem by Patricia Cleghorn

Stop Walking on Eggshells: Taking Your Life Back When Someone You Care About Has Borderline Personality Disorder by Paul T. Mason and Randi Kreger

Wishcraft by Barbara Sher

Maximum Achievement by Brian Tracy

All I Really Need to Know I Learned in Kindergarten by Robert Fulghum

Awake the Giant Within by Anthony Robbins

The Road Less Traveled by M. Scott Peck

A Return to Love by Marianne Williamson

Wisdom In Words

Wisdom In Words

About the Author

The world loves and needs Larry!

So he says; that's why he's decided to spread himself around with a book of 365 inspirational quotes of the day.

Larry Rosenwinkel has a passion for life focusing on "Practical Wellness." He believes in having fun while seeking a balanced lifestyle all the while doing things that inspire and uplift him, whether that be helping others through volunteer work, drinking martinis, traveling, spending time with friends and loved ones, cooking (and eating) or getting on out there doing physical things that contribute to, promote and nurture his overall health and well-being.

Larry has an M.S. in Human Services, a B.A. in English, as well as a Certificate in Drug and Alcohol Abuse Counseling Studies. He is a personal assistant, yoga instructor, four-time marathon finisher, triathlete *and* professional speaker.

 Phew, he's a busy guy!

Wisdom In Words

www.ingramcontent.com/pod-product-compliance
Lightning Source LLC
Chambersburg PA
CBHW021237280526
45784CB00005B/2134